HOW TO BUY A HOME
THAT MAKES YOU HAPPY

Don't just buy a house;
buy a home

Jeni Temen

©2020 by Jeni Temen

All rights reserved. No part of this book may be reproduced in whole or part, or stored in a retrieval system, or transmitted in any form or by any means, electronic, mechanical, photocopying, recording, or otherwise, without the written permission of the author.

ISBN: 978-1-7345015-2-0

Library of Congress Control Number: 2020902825

Printed in Cedarville, California, USA by R Money Club.

The publisher has strived to be as accurate and complete as possible in the creation of this book.

This book is not intended for use as a source of legal, health, medical, business, accounting, or financial advice. All readers are advised to seek the services of competent professionals in legal, health, medical, business, accounting, and financial fields.

The advice and strategies found within may not be suitable for every situation. This work is sold with the understanding that neither the author nor the publisher is held responsible for the results accrued from the advice in this book.

While all attempts have been made to verify information provided for this publication, the publisher assumes no responsibility for errors, omissions, or contrary interpretation of the subject matter herein.

Because of the dynamic nature of the Internet, any web addresses or links contained in this book may have changed since publication of this book and may no longer be valid.

For more information, visit https://www.RMoneyClub.com/

For bulk book orders, contact Jeni Temen at Coach@RMoneyClub.com

Dedication

This book is dedicated to Dan Rider, my first Real Estate Broker, who taught me early on that educating clients was imperative to career success.

Table of Contents

Introduction vii

Chapter 1:   Decide to Buy. 1

Chapter 2:   When is the Best Time to Buy? 13

Chapter 3:   What Kind of House and Where? 17

Chapter 4:   What is Important to You and
What Can You Live Without? 19

Chapter 5:   How Can the Address of Your
New House Affect Your Life and
Happiness? .21

Chapter 6:   How to Choose an Agent 29

Chapter 7:   How to Find a House 31

Chapter 8:   Escrow. 39

Chapter 9:   Closing 43

Chapter 10: Moving In .45

Chapter 11: Buying a Foreclosure. 49

Chapter 12: Buying a Short Sale 57

Chapter 13: Real Estate Investing-A Few Things
for You to Know 59

Chapter 14: Vital Information for the Process 63

              Home Search Requirements. 66

              Home Purchase Checklist 67

              Helpful Links 72

              Escrow Parties List 74

              Title Considerations 76

Glossary of Terms .79

About the Author .87

A Special Bonus Gift from Jeni. 93

Introduction

This book is a short, easy-to-understand guide, written by a real estate professional with nearly 20 years' experience in the real estate world, helping hundreds of clients both buy and sell their homes, land, farms, ranches and investment properties. Inside you'll discover the entire process for buying a house that will make you happy.

Making the wrong decision in buying a home can have devastating and long-lasting effects. On the other hand, making a wise decision when home buying can greatly enhance the overall value of the investment. It is necessary to learn all you can about the world of home buying and mortgages before setting out to purchase the home of your dreams.

When buying a home, it is often best to use a systematic approach, as this is often the best way to be sure that all decisions are based on information and reason, not on impulse or emotion. Buying a home can be an emotional process, nevertheless, it is imperative to keep your emotions under control and not let them cloud your judgment.

How to get the most from this book

Read the entire book first and then come back and work on the scenario you would like to see happen. Use this book as a workbook.

A few extra notes

Throughout this book, I'll give you Western Feng Shui tips for buying a home that fits your desired lifestyle.

If you have a home for sale, check out *"For Sale By Owner. It's not rocket science; just follow the rules."* It explains the entire process of selling a home, with or without an agent.

Chapter 1

Decide to Buy

A lot of people just <u>wish</u> they could buy a house, as opposed to actually being ready to buy a house. They make a habit of going and looking at homes for sale. That might be fun for a weekend outing, but it is not a great way to end up entering into a contract. You will be tempted; you might fall in love with a house and be rushed into placing an offer. This happens way too often, and that's when home buying becomes a very stressful affair, and many times, a bad investment.

Once you are at a point in your life when you think you need to buy a house, stop for a moment and learn whether you want to buy or rent.

Learn what's involved and what to expect. Buying a house is a lot easier than you think, and before you know it, you'll find yourself in debt up to your ears. Being patient and making a smart decision will get you the right house. A house that feels comfortable, brings you luck and becomes a great investment.

So, what does it take to <u>make the decision to buy?</u>

- What kind of market are you in?
- Is it a seller's market or a buyer's market?

I never suggest buying a home in a seller's market. You would pay top dollar in a seller's market, and if the values go down, you're sure to lose. Sometimes you don't have much choice, but you have the choice to be careful and learn the steps.

- Get to know your numbers.
- What kind of loan can you get?
  - A 30-year loan, a 15-year loan, or other.
  - A long-term loan, like a 30 year or longer loan, has a higher interest rate and a lower monthly payment, but the total cost is a lot higher.
  - A shorter-term loan, like a 15-year loan, has a lower interest rate and is cheaper in the long run, but monthly payments are higher.

Here is an example:

$250,000 loan for 30 years at 5% interest

monthly payment: $1342.00

total cost= $483,139.00

$250,000 loan for 15 years at 4.75% interest

monthly payment: $1944.00

total cost= $350,024.00

You'll pay about $133,115.00 less on a 15-year mortgage loan.

There are some ways to pay off a loan faster.

<u>Pay extra toward the principal.</u>

Here is an example:

$250,000, 30-year loan, 5% interest - if you pay $50.00/mo. more towards the principal, you will pay off your house in 27 years and 8 months and save $21,000 in interest payments.

<u>Pay biweekly.</u>

Here is an example:

$250,000, 30-year loan, 5% interest, biweekly payments - you will pay off your loan in 25 years and 3 months and save $43,000 in interest payments.

Other available loans

You can get some creative loans, like a loan for a period of 5 or 7 years with a balloon payment at the end of the period. That would mean you have to come up with a lump sum and pay off the loan.

You can get a loan with an ARM (Adjustable Rate Mortgage). This kind of loan means you have a few years of a guaranteed interest rate. After that time, the interest rate will adjust to the rate available at that time. I would caution against such loans because interest rates are so low right now and they will only go up. A lot of people lost their homes when their rates reset to a high interest rate and they could no longer afford the payments.

A fixed interest rate can't change, so you know what you have to pay for the duration of the loan without any nasty surprises.

There are Conventional Loans, FHA Loans and Special Programs Loans.

Conventional Loans:

- Usually cost less than FHA loans but are harder to get.
- Are not part of any government program.
- Are divided into two categories: **conforming** and **nonconforming.**
    - **Conforming loans** have maximum loan amounts set by the government and have rules set by Fannie Mae and Freddie Mac.
    - **Non-Conforming Loans** are a lot less standardized.

Eligibility varies by lender, and that's why it is advisable to shop around.

Note: Mortgage insurance might be required on either loan if less than a 20% down payment is provided. That is an important item that will add greatly to your mortgage payment and does nothing for you. You might be told that once your home value increases to 120% of the value on the day you purchase, the PMI (Private Mortgage Insurance) will go away. This is not true. It doesn't just go away. You will have to call the mortgage company and get them to agree (good luck on that one). If they agree, they'll order an appraisal, which you will have to pay for. Once the appraisal is complete, if it is indeed higher than 120%, you might get the PMI removed. I have yet to see this happen, even though they are required to do so. I have personally tried for myself and for my clients. It is like talking to the walls and takes many months to years to get responses.

Most people refinance when the house reaches a higher value. That is a viable option, however, it will cost you again. Not every refinance is a good move for you. When a refinance takes place, in most cases, they will start the loan all over again. Think about that before you do it. If you have already paid for several years and now the loan takes you back to the very beginning, who wins? The mortgage company. You need to have the math done and ask for a comparison between the current loan and the new loan.

In Conventional Loans you'll have:

- **Jumbo Conforming** for homes valued at prices higher than the limit.
- **Jumbo Non-Conforming.**
- **Non-Conforming Other.**

All of them are offered at lender's terms and discretion.

FHA or Federal Housing Administration Loans:

- Lower down payment, as low as 3.5%.
- Offered to people with lower credit scores.
- Have a maximum loan amount that varies by County.
- Requires mortgage insurance on all loans.

VA or Veteran Administration Loans:

For veterans, service members and surviving spouses.

Here is the official VA website:

https://www.benefits.va.gov/homeloans/resources_veteran.asp

You need a certificate of eligibility from the VA.

https://www.ebenefits.va.gov/ebenefits/about/feature?feature=cert-of-eligibility-home-loan

- No down payment unless required by the lender or the purchase price is more than the reasonable value of the property.
- No private mortgage insurance premium requirement.
- VA rules limit the amount you can be charged for closing costs.
- Closing costs *may* be paid by the seller.
- The lender can't charge you a penalty fee if you pay the loan off early.
- VA may be able to provide you some assistance if you run into difficulty making payments.
  - You don't have to be a first-time home buyer.
  - You can reuse the benefit.
  - VA-backed loans are assumable, as long as the person assuming the loan qualifies.

USDA Loans or Rural Development Loans:

- Offered to low and moderate-income borrowers in rural areas.
- No down payment necessary, but mortgage insurance is required.

State and Local Programs:

Many states and non-profit local agencies offer programs designed to offer assistance to low income borrowers. You can check the link below for available down payment programs in your area, but don't get persuaded into hiring a Realtor or loan officer suggested by the website. They get kickbacks, which ultimately come out of your pocket. Keep on reading and you'll learn how to hire the right agent to benefit just you.

https://downpaymentresource.com/

Special Loans:

Available to teachers, firefighters, and EMTs to buy a home for 50% less. https://www.teachernextdoor.us/Home

First time home buyer or buyers who receive local program help:

Find a HUD approved housing counselor in your area and get your counseling certificate because you will need it. Do it as soon as possible because you might have trouble getting an appointment for the next class. Classes are not always available either.

https://www.consumerfinance.gov/find-a-housing-counselor/

Owner Carry Financing:

Once in a while you'll find a house where the owner wants to carry the contract. That means the owner is using it as an investment. There is nothing wrong with that as long as you get a competitive interest rate and terms. Many times, owner carry loans have a much higher interest rate than the bank offers and the terms are very different. Seldom will you find an owner carry loan for 30 years. Usually they carry for 5, 7, or 10 years, and then you have to refinance - unless you sell it before that time.

If you decide to accept owner carry terms, make sure there is no prepayment penalty clause. (That means if you pay the loan off early you will pay a penalty. That can hurt if you want to refinance or sell). Be careful that there is no lien on the property when you buy on owner carry terms. Sometimes there are liens not yet recorded or recorded so late that they will not show in the title. Have the seller sign a note stating there is no lien of any kind on the property, and if any appear after the sale of the property, they will take full responsibility.

Note: Some home sellers don't understand what owner carry means, and they think they can sell a house on owner carry terms while they still have a mortgage, whether first, second, or sometimes third or more against the house. That is a huge no no. You should NOT get into such a mess! Only a property clear of any mortgage and clear of any liens can be sold on owner carry terms.

Explore current interest rates for your state.

https://www.consumerfinance.gov/owning-a-home/explore-rates/

Non-US Citizens Loans:

- International borrowers have limited options, but some banks offer non-citizen loans to purchase a home or use as an investment.
- Usually the non-US citizen has to put a down payment of 30% or more.
- One of the banks offering this service is HSBC.

Now that you've learned about the most common loans, you need to decide which one will benefit you the most.

No matter what loan you'd like to apply for, you need to gather your personal and financial information.

This is what you need:

- Pay stub for the last 30 days.
- W-2 forms, last two years.
- Signed federal tax return, last two years.
- Documentation of any other sources of income.
- Bank statements, two most recent.

- Documentation of the source of your down payment: investment or savings account statements showing at least two months' history of ownership. If some of the funds were a gift, get a signed statement from the giver stating that the funds were a gift.
- Documentation of name change, if recent.
- Proof of your identity (typically a drivers' license or non-driver ID).
- Social security number.
- Certificate of housing counseling or home buyer education (if you go for a first-time home buyer loan or get down payment assistance).

What does your credit score say about you? Have you checked your credit lately?

It is imperative to know your credit, not only your score but how it reads. You can check your credit free of charge once a year at https://www.annualcreditreport.com

See if you have anything derogatory, meaning late payments or anything listed in red. If you do, make a note of it and be ready to answer what it is. In case you already paid that delinquency, write a letter to the reporting agencies and explain what happened.

This is called a letter of dispute. You will find that link on your credit report.

The better your credit looks, the lower the interest rate on your loan will be. Even if you have plenty of money as a down payment, the credit score and what the credit report says about your behavior matters.

Ok, now that you have an idea about what kind of loan you would like to go for and how much money you will put as a down payment, you have money for closing costs and you have a three month savings, you're ready to start looking for a house, right?

Not so fast.

Check the calculator to estimate how much your monthly payment can be. You should stay between 30% to 35% of your net income in mortgage payments, otherwise you will have a financial struggle. Here is a calculator:

https://www.calculator.net/loan-calculator.html

Note: In addition to the loan you are getting, you need to take into consideration homeowner association fees, if the house has one. The fees can be huge, and if an association has a pool, the fees can increase sky high over time. I've seen fees increase from $68/mo. to $480/mo. in just three years.

Chapter 2

When is the Best Time to Buy?

The best month to buy a house is January. Not many people are out after the holidays looking for a house. They are busy exchanging or returning gifts and cleaning up the holiday remains. Homes on the market in January have usually been on the market for a while and there is less competition, making room for negotiation. People are also more eager to sell after all the holiday spending.

The worst month to buy is April. People are expecting the tax returns and just like flower buds are coming out in the spring, so are buyers. Competition is fierce and prices are higher.

If you can control when you can make an offer, chose January. If you cannot control when to purchase, maybe you can at least avoid April.

Now you're ready and you know what kind of loan will appeal to you the most.

Contact a local mortgage company and first ask if they do the specific loan you decided on. Tell them specifically NOT to check your credit. This is very important, and they might not respect your request. Be firm and make sure they understand that at this time, you only want to know if they have the specific loan you would like to have. Not every mortgage company has all the loans I listed above. In many cases, if they don't have that product, they will try to convince you it is not that good of a loan for you and you should get one they do have. Don't fall for that. Keep checking with other local mortgage companies and insist, again and again, that they <u>do not check the credit.</u>

Once you are connected with a loan officer, you give them permission to check your credit and you provide the paperwork they require. They will give you a Pre-Approval letter once they receive the credit report. That letter is not a promise that you will receive a loan. It is a letter indicating that you connected with a loan officer and, according to what they know so far, you MIGHT be able to get a loan.

Note: Don't go to several loan officers and apply to see who will give you a better option. DON'T go to online places where they guarantee you a loan. Doing so will mess up your credit instantly because everyone will check your credit and that will lower your credit score. I've seen some of the online companies check people's credit 20 or more times in one phone call. That's because they submit the info to a lot of companies they're working for. What I'm suggesting is, find a mortgage company and stick with them from the beginning to the end. If you do not give them your SS, they can't check your credit!

Chapter 3

What Kind of House and Where?

Be sure to search for a home that really fits your way of life and that you are comfortable with.

A good example of this is if you're working in an office, a good place to find is near or in the vicinity of your office.

If you love nature, a good place to find is outside the city, a place with clean air that is near parks, has a mountain view or is near the beach.

Make sure to look at its suburbs first and try to gather some information about the area and its surroundings.

Try to consider the kind of neighbors you will have.

If you have children, schools might be important.

If you have family in the area, you may like to find a place near them.

Are prices matching the area with your checkbook? Check prices in areas where you want to live.

Use www.Zillow.com to check prices.

Note: When you start searching online for properties and enter information, you will be immediately persuaded to "choose" an agent. That is a way internet companies are selling leads to agents. It is not advisable to connect with an agent that way. Keep reading and you will learn how to connect with an agent.

Chapter 4

What is Important to You and What Can You Live Without?

Make a list with what is most important to you.

Write everything down: how many rooms, how many baths, garage size, yard size, views - everything that matters to you.

Make a second list with what you can compromise on. If you have a partner, do it together. I have yet to see someone in any price range that gets everything they have on the first list. No matter what, that list always gets compromised. That is just how it works. Having two or three lists is very important and saves a lot of time.

The first list can have everything you would love to have on it. E.g. $235,000, 5 years old or newer, 3br/2bath, granite counters, skylights, wooden floors, stucco siding, metal roof, 5-car garage, landscaped back and front, ¼ acre lot, 18-foot ceilings, views of the city from every room.

The last list should have absolutely necessary items on it, things you can't compromise on.

E.g. $235,000, 3 br/2 bath, 2 car garage, ¼ acre lot.

Chapter 5

How Can the Address of Your New House Affect Your Life and Happiness?

Many people are fascinated with Feng Shui, and for many good reasons. Others generally believe that it is some oriental superstitious set of paradigms on interior design. The Western Feng Shui that we know now is actually comprised of various schools of learning and incorporates the different cultures under which it is housed.

You don't need to believe in Feng Shui; it just works!

The main objective of Feng Shui is to invite all the good things into one's life. If Feng Shui is practiced well, prosperity and success are more easily within reach and you can expect a positive disposition.

We've all heard that location is the key consideration when it comes to real estate, and that is certainly the case. What we haven't heard as much is how important Feng Shui is. We know that some homes "just don't sell," no matter how great the location is, and we wonder why that is. We also hear marketers say things like, "No one knows why some numbers attract more sales than others."

It is not a mystery, it is Feng Shui. That is how it works.

All that being said, I always advise purchasing a home that supports you, your endeavors and your health, but that is also a home that will sell when you decide to do so. Please don't say, "I'll never sell my house." I have heard that hundreds of times in my real estate career, and without fail, I got called to sell it again every time because something changed in their lives. You never know.

Now, let's do an exercise to learn about what kind of house will suit you best.

Take your birth date, add all the numbers and reduce to one number.

E.g. 02-27-1978, 0+2+2+7+1+9+7+8 = 36, 3+6 = 9

In this case, your number is 9. This is your life path number.

Do the same thing with the person who is purchasing with you, if anyone.

Keep that number in mind forever, because that is a very important number for you in many areas of your life.

Note: In this book we will only discuss the buying a house portion of Feng Shui. If you have a house for sale, check out the book I wrote called, *"For Sale By Owner. It's not rocket science; just follow the rules."* The Feng Shui tips in his book are general. For a personalized Feng Shui analysis, send email to coach@ RMoneyClub.com

When you start looking at homes, use the same method on the house number (below).

E.g. 253 Avenue de la Rue. 2+5+3 = 10, 1+0 = 1

If the address has a letter, number it by alphabet.

E.g. 253 C Avenue de la Rue. 2+5+3+3 = 13, 1+3 = 4

Below, I'm going to give you the meaning of each house number when reduced to one number. If your personal reduced number is the same as the reduced house number, the meaning will be further emphasized.

House #1- The mind house is a serious house where you discover your individuality. A fresh start. The house of a leader, a house where independent people who don't mind being alone live. If you'd like to start a business and be completely focused on what you're doing, yet not a business where people have to come to the house, this is the house for that.

House #2- This house is a partnership house. A family house where everyone likes to gather and enjoy life and holidays. Care takers, romance writers, nurses, and doctors would love it here. If you have a family and love your extended family coming to visit, this is the house for that.

House #3- This is a house for highly creative people. A playful, party house where people come, invited or not. A house of hosting and socializing. If you are an artist or in any business that involves artistic, creative anything, this is the house for that.

House #4- The path of a builder. This house is all about hard work, discipline, and perfection. This house might also need a lot of work, constantly. You just finished something and something else needs to be done, or you want to do something else. This is also a house of stability and partnership. If you like to work on home improvements and remodels, this is the house for that.

House #5- This is a great house for a home-based business. A house where things change a lot and fast. If you'd like to have a home-based business where people come in and out, this is the house for that.

House #6- Children, family, harmony, and friends are all welcome in this house. If you like to cook, work for an online business, beautify the home, or raise children, this is the house for that.

House #7- This is the most spiritual house of all. People who need or want to be alone will feel comfortable here. This is a house for painters, romance writers, film editors, healers, astrologers, or anything to do with spirituality of any kind and behind the scene work. Not a house for socializing. If you like solitude, this is the house for that.

House #8- This is the money-making house for strong willed people in high leading positions who are always in control. If you are a strong-willed person and money is highly important to you, this is the house for that.

House #9- Caring for humanity will happen in this house. Very nurturing, with the best hosts. People in the medical field, lawyers, actors, and action heroes can be happy here. If you are a very caring person who just wants everyone to be happy, this is the house for that.

Alright, now let's tie all of this together to work for you.

Keeping your own life path number in mind, check all the numbers above and see what kind of life you would like to have.

Be realistic. Don't think you can make it all work out. It doesn't work that way. Take a moment, a few days, and think about all of this with an open mind. Think about what kind of life you want to have in this house.

For instance, I am a life path #1. I've owned several house #4s and loved them all, but the never-ending work that needed to be done, or that I wanted to do, drained my pocket and energy every time. I love doing home repairs, improvements and decorating, but I didn't have time to do anything else due to the continuous work around the property. I sold each one and made a profit; that's the positive part. I also lived in a house #3 for a short four months. I remodeled the entire house and painted more paintings than ever in my life before or after. It was like a possessed paint brush took control of me. I loved it! I lived in a house #9, and if I invited 30 people for dinner, I would have 80 coming. Without fail I had the biggest parties ever at that house. I lived in a house #7. Even though my life path #1 matches pretty well with #7, I felt alone and depressed very fast. I sold the house quickly too, to a school teacher who is still very happy after many years there. Her life path number is 7.

The next important Feng Shui tip is the location of the house.

If the house is located on a cliff, and behind the house the hill goes down, you will have nothing but financial troubles while living there. Money might come in, but it will go out faster than it arrives, regardless of the house number.

Unfortunately, I know that from personal experience. At that time, I ignored Feng Shui. As I said, you don't need to believe in it, it just works that way.

Another tip is, don't buy a house with the entry on the far-left side of the front of the house, or one that has the entry behind the house. Those homes have a very hard time selling, and I know you will want to sell it sooner or later.

Now you know what kind of loan you will take out, what price you want, and what kind of house you want in what area, plus you are paying attention to house numbers. You are now ready to choose an agent.

Chapter 6

How to Choose an Agent

As a buyer, you don't have to pay a commission to an agent, right?

Yes, that's right, but really think about who is paying for the house? You are. The more commission the agent makes, the less you can negotiate with the seller. The reason I suggested you do all of the above work was to make sure you are educated and can make the agent's life easier. Why? Because that agent will be able to give you back some of the commission in certain ways. This is also why you should not work with an agent that is referred by anyone, especially internet companies. When an agent is referred, that agent needs to pay a considerable amount of commission to the referral party. Find your own agent and ask if they have to pay any referral fees to anyone while working with you.

While the agent can't pay you directly, because it is illegal to pay anyone who doesn't have a real estate license or an attorney license, the agent can pay you something in closing costs at close of escrow.

Chose an agent that works in the area where you are looking to buy. Look up real estate signs and names in that area and call them.

Interview the agent like you are a boss interviewing potential employees. In reality, that agent is your "employee" for the duration of the sale. Make sure you feel confident about the agent's knowledge of the area and that they have experience. It is OK if they are a new agent, as long as you know. Chances are that new agents will work a whole lot harder for you. But, pay close attention to any agent! After all, it is your house and one of the biggest investments of your life!

Give the agent the criteria you came up with. You don't need to talk about the home numbers because that's personal to you.

You can explain that you are ready: you have a prequalification letter and you know which houses and locations you like. You can also tell the agent that you are going to make it easy and that you expect some closing costs to be covered. The agent will be happy to help out.

Once you established an agent-buyer relationship, the agent will send you a list of homes to look at. Choose the homes you would like to look at, and before you go, tell the agent you would like to have the property disclosure. That disclosure will tell you if it is worth looking at or not.

Chapter 7

How to Find a House

Things to pay attention to when looking at homes:

You will have a home inspection, but there are things you should quietly notice in order to make your decision to buy and to have more power to negotiate. Please don't start questioning everything. That will put the seller off, and you might not get a chance to submit an offer even if you decide to for that house. Take mental notes of everything you see, and when the time comes, ask the agent to give you some answers.

- Check windows and notice if there is any fogging.
- If the house is on well water, check inside the toilet tank to see if the water is clean or full of iron.
- Look underneath sinks to see if there is any visible water damage or mice droppings.
- Look closely in corners of the house, inside and out, to see if there is any sawdust powder (that can indicate termites).

- Pay attention to any fresh paint. Most of the time people paint over dirty walls or fix holes from frames, that's OK. Other times, they are hiding something, like water damage to the wall from a rainy season. That will come back as soon as it rains again. This happens mostly on homes with basements or on ceilings where the roof is compromised. A home inspector can miss this if the weather has been dry for a while.
- Pay attention to musty smells in the house. That can mean there is a mold infection somewhere that is not visible.
- Pay attention to other odors in the house.
- Pay attention to pet stains on the carpet. You might have to replace the carpet. If you see a brand-new carpet, make sure you ask if the pad was replaced too, and ask for proof of that. If there were pet stains and the pad wasn't removed, the stains and smells will penetrate back into the carpet.
- Take a look at cabinets all over the house and see if you can live with them or if you have to replace them. Consider the cost if you are thinking of replacing. Same with appliances.
- If the cabinets have just been repainted, like many are nowadays, ask if it was done professionally or DIY. If they weren't done right, that paint can

come off within months. A good idea is to get paint samples for touch ups.

- If the house is old, see what kind of power is installed. Ask if it has been upgraded.
- If the house is old, there might be asbestos tiles on the floor. See if any are broken.

Note: You should not remove asbestos by yourself, unless you know how to do that safely.

- Look closely around the water heater and water tank (if it has one). See if there is any visible corrosion.
- Notice broken fencing.
- If the house has a well, check the location of the well head to make sure it is accessible in case of repair needs. Many times the well was put in and after that a bunch of trees were planted. Now that the trees are old, a big rig can't access the well anymore. Also, the trees may actually live on that well water now, and so the static level can go down more and more every year. That means sooner or later the well will need to be deepened. That is a high expense.
- If the house has septic, ask for the location of the tank and leach field. It CANNOT be close to or go the direction of the well.

- Is there a pool? Inground? If above the ground, will it stay? Do you want it to stay? Consider the extra and possibly significant water expense for a pool.
- Is there a hot tub? Will it stay? Do you want the tub to stay or be removed?
- What will stay with the house? Which appliances will stay, and which will not?
- Does the house have a crawlspace or basement? Take a quick look under there to see how accessible it is.
- Does the house sit on a concrete pad? If yes, do you see big cracks around the house?
- Do you see intrusive vegetation against the house? Like bamboo? Or tree roots? They can damage the foundation, and for sure the septic if there is one at the property.
- If the house is not in a subdivision, ask for survey corners.
- Ask for CCR's, if any, and read them before you write an offer. You want to know what you can or can't do. You also want to know how much the dues are. As I mentioned in a previous chapter, be aware that fees can increase, and usually do increase. You HAVE to pay association fees, or the association has the right to put a lien on your

house and ultimately take it from you. It takes only one person to sue the association for the fees to be transferred to the homeowners. Even if the association didn't do anything wrong, attorneys will be paid. People are like that; they will sue without thinking of the ramification.

- If the home is a manufactured home, ask if anything was remodeled or added. If anything was changed on a manufactured home, you won't get a loan. You can't even replace the cabinets. You can replace appliances and windows.
- Anything that looks strange or unknown to you, just ask the realtor to find out what it is.
- Is it a log home? If yes, is it in an area where the humidity in the air compliments the logs? I've seen log homes being built in dry states where log homes have a lot of problems due to lack of humidity. Such logs require extensive and continuous care.

Once you find the house you like and can afford, you're ready to make an offer.

- Don't be too strong, whether making a lowball offer or paying too much.
- Before you write an offer, ask for the Seller Real Property Disclosure. Read that and see what's disclosed and if you're OK with the issues disclosed.

If there are any structural issues, you might not be able to get a loan.

- Ask the realtor to give you a price opinion.
- Think of anything that might need repairs or to be replaced according to your visual observation.
- Ask for average utility bills before you make an offer. If the house is not well insulated, you might be slammed with huge utility bills.
- Make an offer that is not insulting, but not full price. Even if you love the house so much that you're afraid of losing it, the fact that you are already prequalified and prepared makes you a good candidate. I never suggest overbidding on a house. I've watched too many people do that only to feel sorry later on. Some homes just receive many offers, especially #9 homes and homes that have the entryway on the right side of the house and have good Feng Shui.
- Don't ever overpay. Your house is also your investment.

Besides the purchase price, there are other costs that you need to discuss and decide who will pay for:

- Payment for repairs required by lenders (Yes, the lender will require structurally sound homes, therefore necessary repairs will need to be made before closing).

- Payments for transfer tax.
- Payment for title search.
- Payment for title insurance.
- Payment for recording fees.
- Payment for escrow fees.
- Payment for surveys.
- Payment for inspections: home inspection, termites, septic, well, water quality/quantity, pool, etc.
- Payment for reinspection, if needed.

If you ask the seller to pay for a lot of closing costs, you won't be able to get the total purchase price too far down.

A seller is also interested in how fast you can close. The faster you can close, the better for the seller, except in same very isolated cases.

Have your realtor negotiate for you and give one day to receive a response. Don't insist on a faster response because it is always helpful when people have the night to think about it. Don't give too much time, because people will rethink and can receive other offers. Your realtor will know all that. Now is the time to ask the realtor for some concessions. You can ask for certain things to be paid by the realtor at close of escrow - things like home warranty, a certain amount to be credited towards the closing costs, and anything you and the realtor agree upon. If you **didn't** pick a realtor who is referred by someone and needs to pay a hefty referral fee, that realtor will be very happy to pay for some of your closing costs. Remember, it is illegal for a Realtor to pay you money directly. It has to go through escrow.

Chapter 8

Escrow

Once your offer is accepted, your realtor will open escrow with your earnest money deposit check.

At this point, time is of the essence, and your realtor will keep track to make sure that everything is done according to the contract. If you don't have a realtor, but the seller has a realtor, you can work with that realtor.

Be aware though that a seller's realtor will be representing the seller, not you. That doesn't mean they will not do a good job; however, you need to be on top of your game. Read what is handed to you to sign, and question it if something is not clear.

If neither you nor the seller has a realtor, ask the seller how they were going to proceed. If they don't have a process in mind, but insist on not using a realtor, my book, *"**For Sale by Owner. It's not rocket science; just follow the rules**,"* explains exactly how the seller who doesn't want a realtor can proceed. It is available on Amazon in print and as an eBook. The eBook is free, or almost free, and print is $9.99. The information is definitely worth reading.

I can imagine a seller will not just decide to sell a house without a plan, but, if they don't have a plan, I suggest you check out that book and learn what they would have to offer you. At the end of the book, you'll find a suggested contract and links for every state contract, too. Don't rush into buying a home from a seller who doesn't have representation and is not prepared. Remember, it is a big investment and you don't want to be stuck with a bad purchase. If you prefer to hire an attorney, be sure that attorney is knowledgeable about real estate purchases. Just because they have a law degree doesn't mean they know real estate. I've represented attorneys selling their own homes in the past.

Don't let anyone rush you in any part of this process!

You will have inspections and appraisals done. Don't ever waive inspections! Even if you pay with all cash and want to close really fast, you need to know if the house is sound. Also, an inspector has liability for the inspection they deliver.

Note: If you decide to be present at inspection time, DO NOT interfere with the way the inspector does the work. Don't point out anything and don't ask any questions. Doing so, you'll release the inspector from liability, and if something is wrong or missed by the inspector, you won't have a case.

It's a common practice that the inspector will turn to the buyer (if the buyer is present) after they finish the inspection and explain the major findings. You can ask questions at that time.

If you're not there, which is always the best option, once you receive the inspection report you can call the inspector if you have questions.

According to the findings, you might ask for various things to be repaired. I always suggest to only ask for items needed to satisfy the loan (like leaks and roof repairs). Everything else is better to take care of yourself once you own the house. Why? Because the seller will do, or have done, repairs on the cheap and in a hurry in order to hand the property over to you. When it is up to you, you will have everything done the right way because it is your house. It is best if you negotiate a better price. If you have more repairs than you expected, you can ask the realtor to write an addendum asking for money in lieu of repairs. E.g. in lieu of repairs, seller to credit buyer $X… at close of escrow.

Inspections, appraisals, and loans all need to be done according to the timeline in the contract. If any deadline is missed and not addressed in an addendum, the contract will become null and void. That means if an inspection or appraisal or loan officer needs more time than the contract states prior to the specific deadline, the issue needs to be addressed. E.g. a pest inspector can't come on the specific date, but two days later. Write an addendum asking for two more days to accommodate the inspection.

The most common delay is always the loan officer. They like to work in the last few days, when all inspections are done and they know the house, as well as the borrower, qualifies for the loan.

Note: It's highly important that you not do ANYTHING that will compromise your credit during the time you are in escrow.

So many people get prequalified and rush to buy furniture, cars, etc., only to end up with a lot less of a money cushion by the time escrow closes. The loan officer has to check your credit again right before the loan gets funded. You would be surprised to know how many escrows don't close because the bank won't fund them after that spending. Getting angry at that time will not help either. My advice is to wait until the loan closes before you shop for whatever you have planned. During escrow, more saving than less is always a good thing. The lender wants to see a cushion in your bank account.

At the end of escrow, once the loan is all approved, you will be asked to go and sign papers at the escrow/title company.

Chapter 9

Closing

Usually the seller signs first, but it doesn't matter if they didn't sign before you. You will be shown the settlement pages where you should verify all numbers to make sure they are conforming to the contract. Mistakes are made all the time. Check the title information and ask questions if you don't understand something. Check the numbers and see if they reflect what the realtor promised to pay. If not, have the escrow agent call and redo the numbers.

After everyone signs and the loan is approved and ready to be funded, you have two days to close. This is the time for a final walk through. A final walk through is required for your protection. You, the buyer, need to see if your future house still has everything that you saw and agreed with the last time you visited. Many times sellers will take appliances out and replace them with cheaper ones, or replace light fixtures or promised furniture, etc. You now have the opportunity to see if that's the case or not. Should such a thing happen, you have the right to either cancel the contract and walk away or ask for monetary reimbursement before closing escrow. In such a case, everything still has to go through escrow. This is something that happens mostly in cases where realtors are not involved.

If everything is the way you expected, that gives the escrow officer the green light to complete the closing.

Chapter 10

Moving In

During this time, many buyers want to start moving things in. It starts with just one box, then another one, and so on. **This is NOT a good idea, even if the seller is OK with the idea.** Your insurance won't kick in until your closing day, when the title of the house gets transferred to your name. On the flip side, the seller's insurance is not covering you either. Please don't think that accidents don't happen, because they do. Also, you have no control over who is visiting the property or when during this volatile time. So much can happen; things can get stolen and people can get injured. Please wait until the closing happens and you receive the keys from the seller.

If you can, make another trip to the house prior to the moving van arriving, just to make sure the seller left the house, the house is clean, no trash was left behind and all items you agreed to are still there.

What happens if the house is not cleaned and a lot of stuff was left behind?

You have options:

- Call the seller, or the Realtor if you worked with one, and insist they have to comply. This usually resolves it.
- Complain to the real estate division, if a Realtor was involved, and file a complaint. This involves a lot of paperwork and time.
- If no Realtor was involved, you can go to the small claims court and file a complaint.
- Take care of it yourself.

Things to do after you receive the keys to the house, garage door and mailbox:

- You NEED to change the locks on every door! Never skip this step! A lot of people were in and out of this house, especially during escrow. Change the garage door code, too. Don't leave this step to chance!
- Have the electricity scheduled to be transferred to your name. This needs to be done a few days early to make sure you're not without power while you're moving.

- Have the water scheduled to be transferred in your name, and make sure if the water was off, that you are in the house when it is turned back on. Some faucets might have been left on or sprinklers might start running.
- Have the gas company scheduled to do the transfer, and make sure you're home when it gets turned on as well. You could have a burner on and come home to an explosion.
- Set up the trash account.
- Set up internet service.
- Set up your new address with the post office.
- Change your address with your banks and credit card companies.

Take a moment for yourself and your loved ones and breathe!

Appreciate your accomplishment and thank the universe for helping you get there! You're starting a brand-new chapter in your life. Be intentional!

Chapter 11

Buying a Foreclosure

A foreclosure means the lender on a property's loan took the title due to non-payment. Every state has its own foreclosure laws.

Buying a foreclosure can be a very good investment, but it can also be a very bad one. Being careful is imperative. It doesn't matter if you have a realtor or not, you HAVE to be very diligent.

From the very beginning you will be asked to sign document after document, and each one will release someone of liability. Someone besides the buyer. There is no document that guarantees you anything.

This list gives you a brief look at what to expect in each state:

1. State
2. Judicial
3. Non-Judicial
4. Process Time in Days

5. Publish Sale in Days
6. Redemption Time – in Days
7. Sale by

1	2	3	4	5	6	7
Alabama	Y	Y	49-74	21	365	Trustee
Alaska	Y	Y	105	65	365	Trustee
Arizona	Y	Y	90+	41	30-180	Trustee
Arkansas	Y	Y	70	30	365	Trustee
California	Y	Y	117	21	365Y	Trustee
Colorado	Y	Y	145	60	None	Trustee
Connecticut	Y	N	62	N/A	Court	Court
Delaware	Y	N	170-210	60-90	None	Sheriff
Florida	Y	N	135	N/A	None	Court
Georgia	Y	Y	37	32	None	Trustee
Hawaii	Y	Y	220	60	None	Trustee
Idaho	Y	Y	150	45	365	Trustee
Illinois	Y	N	300	N/A	90	Court
Indiana	Y	N	261	120	None	Sheriff
Iowa	Y	Y	160	30	20	Sheriff
Kansas	Y	N	130	21	365	Sheriff
Kentucky	Y	N	147	N/A	365	Court
Louisiana	Y	N	180	N/A	None	Sheriff
Maine	Y	N	240	30	90	Court
Maryland	Y	N	46	30	Court	Court
Massachusetts	Y	N	75	41	None	Court
Michigan	N	Y	60	30	30-365	Sheriff

1	2	3	4	5	6	7
Minnesota	Y	Y	90-100	7	180	Sheriff
Mississippi	Y	Y	90	30	None	Trustee
Missouri	Y	Y	60	10	365	Trustee
Montana	Y	Y	150	50	None	Trustee
Nebraska	Y	N	142	N/A	None	Sheriff
Nevada	Y	Y	116	80	None	Trustee
New Hampshire	N	Y	59	24	None	Trustee
New Jersey	Y	N	270	N/A	10	Sheriff
New Mexico	Y	N	180	N/A	30-270	Court
New York	Y	N	445	N/A	None	Court
North Carolina	Y	Y	110	25	None	Sheriff
North Dakota	Y	N	150	N/A	180-365	Sheriff
Ohio	Y	N	217	N/A	None	Sheriff
Oklahoma	Y	Y	186	N/A	None	Sheriff
Oregon	Y	Y	150	30	180	Trustee
Pennsylvania	Y	N	270	N/A	None	Sheriff
Rhode Island	Y	Y	62	21	None	Trustee
South Carolina	Y	N	150	N/A	None	Court
South Dakota	Y	Y	150	23	30-365	Sheriff
Tennessee	N	Y	40-45	20-25	730	Trustee
Texas	Y	Y	27	N/A	None	Trustee
Utah	N	Y	142	N/A	Court	Trustee
Vermont	Y	N	95	N/A	180-365	Court
Virginia	Y	Y	45	14-28	None	Trustee
Washington	Y	Y	135	90	None	Trustee

1	2	3	4	5	6	7
Washington DC	N	Y	47	18	None	Trustee
West Virginia	N	Y	60-90	30*60	None	Trustee
Wisconsin	Y	Y	290	N/A	365	Sheriff
Wyoming	Y	Y	60	25	90-365	Sheriff

States that use mortgages conduct judicial foreclosures, and states that use deeds of trust conduct nonjudicial foreclosures. The judicial foreclosure means a court action needs to be performed to foreclose a home. Some states use both judicial and nonjudicial foreclosures.

If you look at a house that's in pre-foreclosure, it is important to pay attention to the process period days. As you can see, it varies in each state. This time can become a whole lot longer if the home owner makes a payment from time to time and asks for loan modification or forgiveness. I suggest you do nothing but watch when you spot a home you'd like to buy that is in pre-foreclosure.

If a home/property is already foreclosed and offered for sale again, pay close attention to the redemption period for the state where the property is located. A redemption period means that the former owner has the right to reclaim the title and possession of the property by paying off the debt. Don't assume just because they moved out that it is done and all over with. Many people come back, and if you already purchased the property, you will have to walk out. It happens!

This happens to people who don't read everything and sign blindly. There is a clause in the contract that tells you something similar to "buyer understands the right of redemption."

The best and most secure way to purchase a foreclosed property is to wait until it is listed with a realtor. Once you see it advertised, you can contact the agent who has the property listed and offer to bid. If you would like to use your own realtor, make sure that agent has knowledge about buying foreclosures. That is a very different task than just selling a home. Ask the agent if they have any training in REOs (Real Estate Owned) and how many foreclosures they have worked on successfully. It has to be at least four.

The listing agent on a foreclosed property will have total control of the selling process. Banks only use specifically trained agents to list their assets.

Once you offer your highest and best bid, you have to wait a specific period of time, the time dictated by the REO company. They all have various timeframes for receiving offers. They will look at all offers and go for the best one. The best offer is not necessarily the highest offer. It counts if you pay all cash and close fast.

You have to have a letter stating exactly how you will purchase the property. If you have all cash, a letter from the bank needs to be presented at time of offer. If you want to take out a loan, a full approval letter needs to be presented with the offer.

Once your offer is accepted, you need to do your own due diligence. Regardless of if you have a realtor or not, do your work. Have inspections done in order to know what you're getting into. I've seen many homes with issues like concrete poured into the pipes, broken sewer lines, broken main water lines, holes in the walls, holes in the floor, flooded crawlspace, broken kitchens, etc.

I personally purchased two homes with issues, but because I knew about them, I was able to negotiate the price even lower and ended up with a very good deal. When a foreclosed home has big issues, you have a big chance to get it with all cash. That's because no bank will finance it, and the property has to go with all cash.

Like I already mentioned, make sure you ask about the redemption period and if it has passed. I also suggest purchasing extra title insurance to cover unseen title issues. Your escrow agent can guide you on what is available.

Go to the city or county where the property is located and find out if there are any new liens on the property. If a property is listed with an asset manager, usually they took care of the title and liens. Just be sure that is the case.

If you have cash to purchase foreclosures, and an interest in repairing and sparkle cleaning, you can end up with a great investment.

Chapter 12

Buying a Short Sale

A short sale is a way of selling homes/properties that are underwater. That means the homeowner owes more money to the bank than the house is worth. When the lender is willing to sell the house for less than the homeowner owes, that becomes a short sale.

A short sale is a great purchase if you have plenty of time to wait. It takes many months for a short sale to get approved, and it requires 100% cooperation from the sellers. Everyone who's name is on title needs to cooperate and submit a lot of paperwork on time. There can be two or three banks involved, and each one has to approve and accept the short sale. During the last recession, I saw short sales in the process for as many as five years. It all depends on the seller's willingness to let the house go. Many of them don't want to go because they have stayed in the house without paying for a while and don't have a place to go.

That's the negative part. You can wait and wait, and then the homeowner can receive a loan modification and keep the property.

In other cases, if the seller cooperates, you can make an offer with an agent. Again, only use an agent who has experience with short sales or go to the listing agent.

Once the offer is accepted, it will go just like any regular sale.

The sellers have the responsibility to take care of the house until it closes, otherwise the lender will foreclose on them. There is a significant difference on the seller's credit report. A short sale is a lot easier to survive than a foreclosure. That is the incentive. Banks don't want to foreclose because it costs a lot of additional money and trouble, and sellers usually don't want a foreclosure on their credit report.

You can finance a short sale the same way you finance any home. Please don't wave inspections to save money. It might be a good chunk at the time of purchase, but at least you know what you're getting.

I suggest you purchase an additional title insurance. Check with the escrow officer on what they can offer you to protect your title.

Chapter 13

Real Estate Investing-A Few Things for You to Know

I don't know of any wealthy person who doesn't own real estate! That's because real estate can be a very lucrative investment, but only if you do it right.

You can lose a lot of money in real estate, too, just like in any other investment.

Here are just a few tips for you to think about before you purchase.

- What kind of property?
- Are you thinking of a house? Or a parcel of bare land? Or a commercial property?
- If it is a house, is it in a neighborhood where people like to rent?
- How much money can you rent it for?
- Does it have association fees? A house with association fees can make a huge dent in your investment.

- Are you going to manage the house yourself? Or do you need a property manager? If you intend to manage yourself, check the State Laws and make sure you comply. Some states require a property manager to be less than a certain number of miles away from the property. Having a property manager costs money, too.

- If you think to purchase a parcel of land, is it located in a developing area? Does it have access to utilities? Does it need a well? How long can you hold the land to hope for an increase in value? A piece of land can be a great and inexpensive long-term investment if located in an area where people would want to live or build something. For instance, if a big development is in progress in an area, check areas surrounding and pay attention to what the master plan is. You could snap a cheap parcel and make three to four times in profit if you pay attention. It can also be 40 years of nothing but waiting if you purchase land without knowing anything about the area. A lot of people buy land online because it looks good on paper. You want to always *always* walk the land and ask yourself, "What will I do with this land if it never sells?" If your answer is, "I could live here," or, "I can see a need for a commercial building here," then you can start due diligence and find out what the city or county has in future plans for that area. Zoning is very important. Many past clients of mine made a lot of money in land purchases. Be very selective on land purchases and you can make money, too.

How are you going to pay for it?

Paying cash for a piece of real estate for investment purposes is always the best idea. If you need to take out a loan, put at least 30% down. That way you will get a better rate. If you don't have enough for the down payment, rethink the purchase as an investment.

Will it be a long-term or short-term investment?

- For a long-term investment in a home, you need to think tenants.
- For a short-term investment in a home, you need to think repairs and flipping. That is very lucrative if you have cash and can purchase run down, trashed, or foreclosed homes. You would fix them, clean them and resell them.

If you want to resell on owner carry terms, you can do that if you don't have a loan on the property and if you don't mind having your money tied up for a few years. Most owner carry terms are for 5, 7, or 10 years, amortized for 30 years with a balloon payment at the end of the contract. You would have to be competitive with the interest rate, but think about where else you can get such a great return. I think this is a much better option than renting because the person who buys the property will take care of the property and pay taxes and insurance, and you just get the payments.

The problem arises when the buyer stops making payments. To prevent that, you need a good contract that protects you from going into foreclosure. I suggest a clause that states if the buyer misses a payment for more than 60 days or defaults on taxes, they are obligated to return the title to seller without the process of foreclosure. Have an attorney draft such a contract for you, a real estate attorney that is.

If you are looking at a commercial property, it is best if you contact a commercial real estate broker. Purchasing a commercial property is a lot more involved and I never advise such investment without a pro. You might want to consult an attorney, too, but be sure it is a real estate attorney.

<u>Perhaps the best advice I can give you in investing in real estate in general is:</u>

Don't purchase real estate in a state, or even in an area, you don't know anything about!

Always buy in an area you know well and can go see at any time of the day or night if necessary.

Chapter 14

Vital Information for the Process

Home Search Worksheet
Realtor interview

Name . . . .   ph . . . .

email . . . .

website . . . .

What experience do you have in this area?.

. . . .
. . . .
. . . .
. . . .

What kind of properties have you sold the most?

. . . .
. . . .
. . . .
. . . .
. . . .

Do you have experience in selling homes with land? (if you're looking at a home with land)

．．．．．．．．．．．．．．．．．．．．．．．．．．．．．．．．．．．．
．．．．．．．．．．．．．．．．．．．．．．．．．．．．．．．．．．．．
．．．．．．．．．．．．．．．．．．．．．．．．．．．．．．．．．．．．

Have you sold any foreclosures? (if you're looking at buying a foreclosure)

．．．．．．．．．．．．．．．．．．．．．．．．．．．．．．．．．．．．
．．．．．．．．．．．．．．．．．．．．．．．．．．．．．．．．．．．．
．．．．．．．．．．．．．．．．．．．．．．．．．．．．．．．．．．．．

Have you sold any short sales? (if you are looking at buying a short sale)

．．．．．．．．．．．．．．．．．．．．．．．．．．．．．．．．．．．．
．．．．．．．．．．．．．．．．．．．．．．．．．．．．．．．．．．．．
．．．．．．．．．．．．．．．．．．．．．．．．．．．．．．．．．．．．

Have you sold any condominiums? (if you're looking to buy a condominium)

．．．．．．．．．．．．．．．．．．．．．．．．．．．．．．．．．．．．
．．．．．．．．．．．．．．．．．．．．．．．．．．．．．．．．．．．．
．．．．．．．．．．．．．．．．．．．．．．．．．．．．．．．．．．．．

Explain how you are going to work with me

．．．．．．．．．．．．．．．．．．．．．．．．．．．．．．．．．．．．
．．．．．．．．．．．．．．．．．．．．．．．．．．．．．．．．．．．．
．．．．．．．．．．．．．．．．．．．．．．．．．．．．．．．．．．．．

Will you be willing to help me with closing costs if I make your experience easy and if you don't pay any referral fees to others?

. . . .
. . . .
. . . .

Supervising broker

Name . . . .

Office number . . . .   Cell . . . .

email . . . .

Home Search Requirements

Price range. . . . .

Area . . . .

Rooms #. . . . .

Baths # . . . .

SF . . . .

Lot/land size . . . .

Garage size . . . .

Age of home . . . .

Specifics

. . . .

. . . .

Additional comments

. . . .

. . . .

. . . .

. . . .

. . . .

. . . .

Home Purchase Checklist

Address . . . .

APN (area parcel number) . . . .

Zoning . . . .   what kind? . . . .

Any zoning issues to be aware of? . . . .

Year built . . . .

Lot size . . . .

House size . . . .

Association . . . .

if yes,

Name . . . .

Phone . . . . Dues . . . . mo./yr.

Website . . . .

Property tax . . . .

City . . . . County . . . .

Is the property subject to private transfer fee? . . . . . .

Any supplemental tax? . . . .

Parcel map No . . . . (request) Y   N

Any encroachments? . . . .

Any future developments known? . . . .

What school district. . . . .

Any noise, odors or nuisance to be aware of? (e.g.: trains, buses, airport, meat processing farms, etc.) . . . .

Any restrictions other than CCR's?. . . . .

Is it in the floodplain? . . . .

Any lead-based paint on the property? . . . .

Any mandatory water cutbacks or shortage? . . . .

Mineral rights . . . . if yes . . . . . . amount . . . . . .

Water rights . . . . if yes . . . . amount . . . .

Water meter. . . . .

Water treatment system . . . . if yes, lease or owned?

If leased, price. . . . .

Fountain(s) . . . .

Heating . . . . what kind . . . .

Last serviced . . . .

Water heater . . . . last serviced or replaced. . . . . .

Woodburning . . . . if yes, is it legal? . . . .

Any specifics to know about?

....
....
....
....

Fireplace/chimney ....

Oil tank Y N

If yes what type .... location ....

is it legal? ....Y N U

Solar heating .... who owns it ....

any future payments ....

Cooling system................................

Septic .... if yes, what kind and when was last serviced

....
....
....

Well .... if yes, how deep ....

Where located .... last water test ....

Leach field .... if yes where located ....

Last inspected .... what kind ....

Propane . . . . if yes, who owns the tank . . . . . .

Yard sprinkler system . . . . if yes, what kind

Where are controls . . . . any issues . . . .

Alarm system . . . . if yes, owned or leased . . . . . .

If leased, price. . . . .

Satellite . . . . if yes, leased or owned . . . .

If leased, price. . . . .

Electrical system. . . . .

Last updated (if an old home) . . . .

Plumbing . . . . any issues . . . .

Last updated (if an old home)

Foundation . . . . what kind . . . .

Any damage . . . .

Any settling/sliding issues . . . .

Structure . . . . any structural defects . . . .

Roof . . . . what kind . . . .

Last inspected . . . . any issues . . . .

Siding . . . . what kind . . . . any issues . . . . . .

Radon . . . . .any testing done? . . . .

Survey . . . . last surveyed . . . .

Has the property been the site of a crime, including drug manufacturing . . . . ?

Other . . . .

Other . . . .

Other . . . .

Helpful Links

Environmental issues and concerns : https://www.epa.gov

Lead Base paint: https://www.epa.gov/lead/protect-your-family-lead-your-home

Wood Stoves: https://www.epa.gov/residential-wood-heaters/fact-sheet-summary-requirements-woodstoves-and-pellet-stoves

Radon: https://www.epa.gov/radon/find-information-about-local-radon-zones-and-state-contact-information

Note: Radon is a colorless and odorless gas linked to lung cancer as a second cause of death after smoking. Click on the link above and see how your area is predictably affected by Radon. A radon test is most of the time free or inexpensive, with a kit from a local agency or university. Not advised to skip this test.

Radon mitigation: https://www.epa.gov/radon/guidance-radon-resistant-construction-and-radon-mitigation

Asbestos: https://www.epa.gov/asbestos

Electromagnetic fields: https://www.epa.gov/radtown/electric-and-magnetic-fields-power-lines

Earthquakes: https://www.usgs.gov/products/data-and-tools/real-time-data

Wildfires: https://inciweb.nwcg.gov/

https://www.usgs.gov/products/data-and-tools/real-time-data/wildfire

Noxious weeds, state by state:

https://plants.usda.gov/java/noxComposite

Flood map, put the home address here:

https://msc.fema.gov/portal/home

Escrow Parties List

Realtor . . . .

Name . . . . ph . . . .

email. . . . .
. . . .

Seller . . . .

Name . . . . ph . . . .

email. . . . .
. . . .

Escrow/ title officer . . . .

Name . . . . ph . . . .

email. . . . .

address. . . . .

Escrow number. . . . .

Loan Officer . . . .

Name . . . . ph . . . .

email. . . . .
. . . .

Home Inspector . . . .

Name . . . . ph . . . .

email. . . . .
. . . .

Pest Inspector. . . . .

Name . . . . ph . . . .

email. . . . .
. . . .

Well Inspector . . . .

Name . . . . ph . . . .

email. . . . .
. . . .

Septic Inspector. . . . .

Name . . . . ph . . . .

email. . . . .
. . . .

Roof Inspector . . . .

Name . . . . ph . . . .

email. . . . .
. . . .

Title Considerations

How are you going to vest title?

Do you have a trust? If not, you really should create one.

If you decide to put the property in a trust, you need to provide a copy of the trust to Title company before closing.

If you are married

- As joint tenants – if one party dies, the property passes to the surviving tenant without probate. It can NOT be willed to an heir.
- As community property- for married couples, in case of death property goes to probate, and CAN be willed to an heir.
- As community property with rights of survivorship- in case of death, it doesn't go to probate and CANNOT be will to heir.
- As tenants in common- used by persons buying together but not married- it needs to state the exact percentage of interest in the property of each person. The ownership interest CAN be sold or willed. In case of death it requires probate

- As his or her sole separate property- in case your state is a community property state, it will require the other spouse to convey the interest to the other spouse. Can be willed; it requires probate in case of death
- Always check the state you're buying property and the state you are a resident to make sure you're doing the best thing for yourself. Ask questions and read small print.

A lot of mistakes are made in title ownership because people rush to move into the new home without reading everything.

Congratulations and welcome to your new home!

Glossary of Terms

Acre- A measurement of land equal to 43,560 square feet.

Amortization schedule- A table which shows how much of each payment will be applied toward principal and how much toward interest over the life of the loan.

APR or annual percentage rate- This is perhaps the most misunderstood term. Is not the note rate on your loan, it's a value created according to a government formula intended to reflect the true annual cost of borrowing, expressed as a percentage. It works a bit like this but not exactly, so just use this as guideline: deduct the closing costs from your loan amount, then using your actual loan payment, calculate what the interest rate would be on this amount instead of your actual loan amount. You will come up with a number close to the APR. Because you are using the same payment on a smaller amount, the APR is always higher than the note rate on your loan.

Appreciation- The increase in value of a property due to changes in market conditions, inflations, or other causes.

Assessed value- This is not the appraised value! This is the valuation placed on property by a public tax assessor for purposes of taxation.

Assessment- The placing of a value on a property for the purpose of taxation

Assignment- When ownership of your mortgage is transferred from one company or individual to another.

Assumable mortgage- A mortgage that can be assumed by the buyer when a home is sold. Usually, the borrower must "qualify" in order to assume the loan.

Balloon mortgage (or balloon payment)- A mortgage loan that requires the remaining principal balance be paid at a specific point in time. For example, a loan may be amortized as if it would be paid over a thirty-year period but requires that at the end of the tenth year the entire remaining balance must be paid.

Biweekly mortgage- A mortgage in which you make payments every two weeks instead of once a month. The result if that instead of making twelve monthly payments during the year, you make thirteen. This extra payment reduces the time it takes to pay off your loan.

Note: there are independent companies that encourage you to set up bi-weekly payment schedules with them on your existing 30-year mortgage. They charge a set-up fee and transfer fee on each payment. You can save all that money by doing the same thing yourself. Some of this kind of offering can be a spam and they might not send your payment to the lender. Be cautious!

Buydown- This is another misunderstood term. Usually refers to a fixed rate mortgage where the interest rate is "bought down" for a temporary period, usually one to three years. After that time and for the remainder of the loan term, the borrower's payment is calculated at the note rate. In order to buy down the initial rate for the temporary payment, a lump sum is paid and held in an account used to supplement the borrower's monthly payment. There funds usually come from the seller(or some other source) as a financial incentive to induce someone to buy the property. A "lender funded buydown" is when the lender pays the initial lump sum. They can accomplish this because the note rate on the loan (after the buydown adjustments) will be higher than the current market rate. One reason for doing this is because the borrower may get to "qualify" at the start rate and can qualify for a higher loan amount. Another reason is that a borrower may expect they're earnings to go up substantially in the near future, but wants a lower payment right now. Be cautious and do the numbers on this one too.

Cap- Adjustable Rate Mortgages have fluctuating interest rates, but those fluctuations are usually limited to a certain amount. Those limitations may apply to how much the loan may adjust over a certain period of time and are referred to as "caps". Some ARM's, although they may have a life cap, allow the interest rate to fluctuate freely, but require a certain minimum payment which can change once a year. There is a limit on how much that payment can change each year, and that limit is also referred to as a cap.

Chain of title- An analysis of the transfer of title to a piece of property over the years.

Clear title- A title that is free of liens or legal questions as to ownership of the property.

Closing- This has a different meaning in different states. In some states a real estate transaction is not considered "closed" until the documents record at the local recorder's office. In others, the "closing" is a meeting where all of the documents are signed and money exchanges hands.

Closing statement- Also called Settlement Statement, is the summary of all costs. Keep this for your tax filing.

Cloud on title- Any conditions revealed by a title search that adversely affect the title to real estate. Usually clouds on title cannot be removed except by deed, release, or court action.

Common area assessment- In some areas they are called Homeowners association fees. They are charges paid to the homeowner's association by the owners of the individual unit in a condominium or planned unit dev elopement (PUD) and are generally used to maintain the property and are generally used to maintain the property and common areas.

Condominium- A type of ownership in a real property where all of the owners own the property, common areas and buildings together, with the exception of the interior of the unit to which they have title. Often mistakenly referred to as a type of construction or development, it actually refers to the type of ownership.

Condominium conversion- Changing the ownership of an existing building to the condominium form of ownership.eg: hotels sometimes change from room rental to condominium ownership.

Cooperative- A type of multiple ownership in which the residents of a multiunit housing complex own shares in the cooperative corporation that owns the property, giving each resident the right to occupy a specific apartment or unit.

Due-on-sale provision- A provision in a mortgage that allows the lender to demand a repayment in full if the borrower sells the property that serves as security for the mortgage.

Easement- A right of way giving persons other than the owner access to or over a property

Eminent domain- The right of a government to take private property for public use upon payment of its fair market value. Eminent domain is the basis for condemnation proceedings.

Encroachment- An improvement that intrudes illegally on another's property.

Encumbrance Anything that affects or limits the fee simple title to a property, such as mortgages, leases, easements, or restrictions.

Escrow account- Once you close your purchase transaction, you may have an escrow account or impound account with your lender. This means the amount you pay each month includes an amount above what would be required if you were only paying your principal and interest. The extra money is held in your impound account (escrow account) for the payment of items like property taxes and homeowner's insurance when they come due. The lender pays them with your money instead of you paying yourself.

Escrow analysis- Once a year your lender will perform an "escrow analysis" to make sure they are collecting the correct amount of money for the anticipated expenditures. You might have to pay more or less after the analysis is complete, depending on if the property taxes and insurance have increased.

Fixture- Personal property that becomes real property when attached in a permanent manner to real estate. This includes trees and shrubs if planted in soil around the property (not in pots).

Grantee- The person to whom an interest in real property is conveyed (buyer).

Grantor- The person conveying an interest in real property (seller).

Mechanic's lien- Subcontractors or suppliers sometimes will file an encumbrance, or mechanic's lien, against a property to seek payment.

Quit-claim deed- A document that releases a party from any interest in a piece of real estate.

Point- Fees charged by lenders at the time a loan is originated. A point is equal to 1 percent of the total loan amount.

Transfer tax- An assessment by state or local authorities at the time of property changes hands.

Two-step mortgage- An adjustable mortgage with two interest rates, one for the first few years and the other for the remainder of the loan.

Servicer- A firm that collects mortgage payments and manages borrower's escrow accounts.

Shared-appreciation mortgage- A loan that allows a lender or other party to share in the borrower's profits when the home is sold.

Subordinate loan- A second of third mortgage

R-value- A construction term that refers to the resistance of to heat loss. The higher the R-value, the slower the rate of the heat loss.

Radon- A ground generated radioactive gas that seeps into some homes through sump pumps, cracks in the foundation and other inlets. A leading cause of lung cancer.

Waiver- A voluntary relinquishing of certain rights or claims.

Variable rate- An interest that changes with fluctuations in such indexes as the U.S Treasury bill index.

Tap fees- Most companies charge a tap fee for hooking up utilities.

Tax lien- An impediment placed against a property, such as back taxes.

Teaser rate- A low, short term rate offered on a mortgage to entice the borrower.

Title insurance- A policy issued to lenders and buyers to protect any losses because of a dispute over the ownership of a property.

About the Author

With nearly 20 years' experience as a professional Realtor, Jeni has helped hundreds of people buy homes, land, farms, ranches and investment properties until she retired from real estate sales in 2019. She served at not only the local and state levels on various real estate committees, but at the national and global level.

Born in Romania and spending 10 years of her life in Germany, Jeni arrived in the USA in 1988 and purchased her first home in 1989, birthing her education in real estate investing. She has purchased and sold 21 homes and 11 parcels of land for herself, making a profit on each and every one.

Jeni's bigger vision for northern Nevada was put into motion with her leadership in working with REALTORS® to understand cultural differences in buying and selling real estate locally and internationally. She was involved with the Governors' Office on Economic Development and the Northern Nevada Developmental Authority and served as the chair of the Reno/Sparks Association of REALTORS® Global Business Committee. As a Global Presidential Liaison and a

Real estate teacher to REALTORS® worldwide, Jeni brought global real estate investment education to Northern Nevada and received the prestigious Abraham Curry Award in 2015.

She served for five years as the National Association of REALTORS® Presidential Liaison to Romania. With her help, Romania is one of the first Eastern European countries to adopt the principles of organized real estate including the REALTOR® Code of Ethics and a Multiple Listing Service.

Jeni studied various schools of feng shui and chose western feng shui for real estate, which she actively used in each and every real estate transaction, both for herself and for her clients. Feng Shui is the language of harmony. Once you understand it, harmony will always be with you. You don't need to believe in it to experience the benefits.

Numbers, energy and personal directions are all huge influences in our lives and can help us succeed (or create messes with our health, money and happiness).

When you buy a house that is out of harmony with your own energy, you can lose money, get sick, or have something else happen that is troubling. We can make a conscious effort to live in harmony with our environment and eliminate bad energy by balancing our environment with simple Feng Shui remedies. It's actually simple, once we know what to look for.

During the economic downturn in 2008, Jeni became a Hud approved housing counselor and opened a counseling office in Reno. Securing this license required extensive HUD approved education in finances, foreclosure and default counseling, first time home buyer education, renters' laws, credit counseling and reverse mortgages.

Jeni earned many certifications as a leader in real estate, including:

- Real Estate Broker Licensed in Nevada
- Certified International Property Specialist
- Commercial Real Estate
- Business Broker
- Certified Eco Broker (Association of Energy and Environmental Real Estate)
- NeighborWorks Certified Housing Counselor
- HECM- Reverse Mortgage counselor
- Foreclosure Intervention and Default Counselor
- REO certified (real estate owned)
- Bridges Out of Poverty Trainer

She also holds certifications as a Life Coach, Health Coach, and Financial Coach. She has served clients in her capacities as a Foreclosure Intervention and Default Counselor, Certified Loss Mitigation Advisor, Credit Counselor, and Financial Social Worker.

Jeni leads a very busy life but is never too busy to help someone achieve their own success.

She offers the following services:

Credit repair class delivered via phone or internet

You've likely heard of companies that promise to erase the bad credit items from your report to improve your score. They charge several hundred and there is **never** a guarantee (if you read the fine print). You will learn step by step how they do that and receive all the forms to do it yourself.

Contact Jeni at coach@RMoneyClub.com for details.

Feng Shui/Numerology personal analysis

Receive your very own analysis to use forever in everything you do. This includes

- Your personal numbers to use in real estate or anything you do
- Luckiest colors to wear
- Instructions for your home and remedies for successful living
- Your personal sitting and sleeping directions for success
- How to live with your partner or other people living in the same house
- Plus answers to your personal questions

If you'd like your life to go your way, you need to go Feng Shui! Contact Jeni at coach@RMoneyClub.com for details.

Real Estate investing coaching

Every successful person (or most of them) made significant profits in real estate investing. I did too! I can help you be a successful real estate investor even if you don't have a huge amount of money to start with.

Coaching is delivered in a small group webinar or one on one. Reading both books I authored is a prerequisite (this book and *"For Sale By Owner; It's not rocket science, just follow the rules"*).

You can learn more at https://www.RMoneyClub.com/ or email at Coach@RMoneyClub.com.

A Special Bonus Gift from Jeni

Now that you've read *"How to Buy a Home that Makes You Happy"*, you are on your way to understanding exactly how you can buy a home and feel happy and content while living there.

Feng Shui in your home is an invisible influence on your health, wealth, and overall happiness. Order a personalize Feng Shui analysis for only $39.00 (normally $99.00). Send email with this code BB039 to coach@RMoneyClub.com

If you need help with your money management so that you can become debt free, send an email request to coach@rmoneyclub.com

If you have a home to sell, check out my book *"For Sale by Owner; It's not rocket science, just follow the rules"*.

I'm in your corner. Let me know if I can help further.

Here's to the successful purchase of your new home!

Best,
Jeni

www.ingramcontent.com/pod-product-compliance
Lightning Source LLC
Chambersburg PA
CBHW071309040426
42444CB00009B/1944